MY BODY

MY BODY

ARMS AND HANDS

AMY CULLIFORD

T0011480

A Crabtree Roots Plus Book

CRABTREE
Publishing Company
www.crabtreebooks.com

School-to-Home Support for Caregivers and Teachers

This book helps children grow by letting them practice reading. Here are a few guiding questions to help the reader with building his or her comprehension skills. Possible answers appear here in red.

Before Reading:

- What do I think this book is about?
  - *I think this book is about how I use my hands and arms.*
  - *I think this book is about how my arms and hands work.*
- What do I want to learn about this topic?
  - *I want to learn how to make my arms stronger.*
  - *I want to learn about actions I can make with my hands.*

During Reading:

- I wonder why...
  - *I wonder why I have two arms and two hands.*
  - *I wonder why I have fingers.*
- What have I learned so far?
  - *I have learned that my elbows help my arms bend.*
  - *I have learned that my fingers help me feel things.*

After Reading:

- What details did I learn about this topic?
  - *I have learned that arms and hands are parts of my body.*
  - *I have learned that hands can be big or small.*
- Read the book again and look for the vocabulary words.
  - *I see the word **elbow** on page 8 and the word **wave** on page 16. The other vocabulary words are found on page 23.*

You have two **arms**.

They are part of
your **body**.

Arms help you carry things.

Jill uses her arms to carry her books.

Each arm has an **elbow**.

Your elbows help your arms bend.

I use my arms to **hug** my mother!

You have two hands.

Hands can be big or small.

You can use your
hands to move things.

I use my hands to **wave** to my friend!

Each hand has
five **fingers**.

Your fingers help you feel things.

I use my fingers to turn the page!

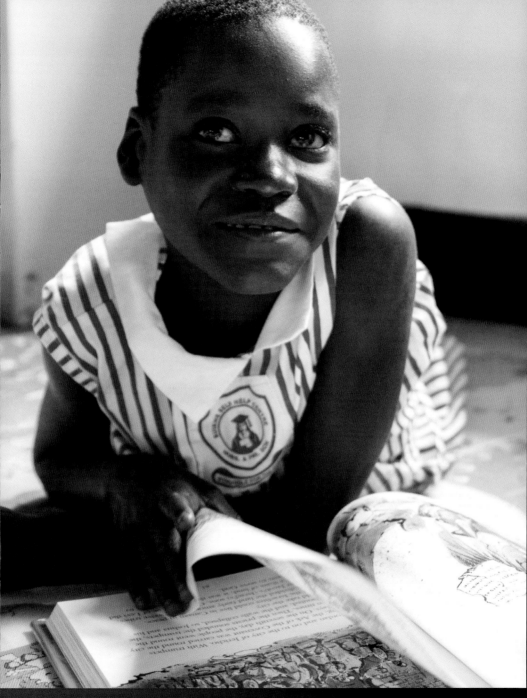

Word List
Sight Words

an	has	the
are	have	they
be	help	things
big	her	to
books	I	turn
can	mother	two
carry	move	use
each	my	uses
feel	of	you
five	or	your
friend	page	
hand	part	
hands	small	

Words to Know

arms

body

elbow

fingers

hug

wave

CRABTREE
Publishing Company

MY BODY
MY BODY HAS
ARMS AND HANDS

Written by: Amy Culliford

Designed by: Rhea Wallace

Series Development: James Earley

Proofreader: Janine Deschenes

Educational Consultant: Marie Lemke M.Ed.

Print and production coordinator:

Katherine Berti

Photographs:
Shutterstock: berezander: cover, p. 3; Pixel-Shot: p. 4; Pressmaster: p.5; wavebreakmedia: p. 7, 16; Olga Chuprina: p. 8; Iakov Filimonov: p. 9; VGStockstudio: p. 11; WEILOKE: p. 12; Aleksandra Belinskaya: p. 13; Hananeko_Studio: p. 15; Studio Kiwi: p. 17

Library and Archives Canada Cataloguing in Publication

Available at the Library and Archives Canada

Library of Congress Cataloging-in-Publication Data

Available at the Library of Congress

Crabtree Publishing Company

www.crabtreebooks.com   1-800-387-7650

Printed in the U.S.A./CG20210915/012022

Copyright © 2022 **CRABTREE PUBLISHING COMPANY**

All rights reserved. No part of this publication may be reproduced, stored in a retrieval system or be transmitted in any form or by any means, electronic, mechanical, photocopying, recording, or otherwise, without the prior written permission of Crabtree Publishing Company. In Canada: We acknowledge the financial support of the Government of Canada through the Canada Book Fund for our publishing activities.

Published in the United States
Crabtree Publishing
347 Fifth Avenue, Suite 1402-145
New York, NY, 10016

Published in Canada
Crabtree Publishing
616 Welland Ave.
St. Catharines, Ontario L2M 5V6